ANGRY BIRDS™
STAR WARS®

CHARACTER ENCYCLOPEDIA

Written by Steve Bynghall and Glenn Dakin

Contents

In a galaxy far, far away, there is a lot of action. The evil pigs are hungry for power and tasty junk food. Porky leaders like Darth Swindle and Lard Vader are constantly attacking groups of angry Bird Rebels. These greedy swine seek something that holds the power to rule the universe... The Egg. But the birds are puzzled—they don't have any eggs! Only Yoda Bird knows where The Egg is hidden!

In this time of civil war and great unrest, the bravest birds emerge to fight back. Jedi Birds such as Red Skywalker and Obi-Wan Kaboomi, leaders like Queen Peckmé Amidala, and lovable rogues like Chuck Solo are among the feathered heroes and heroines risking their all. Can good triumph over porkiness?

BIRD REBELS AND JEDI

BIRD REBEL LINE-UP

RED SKYWALKER

BLUE SQUADRON

LANDO BIRDISSIAN

PECKMÉ AMIDALA

CAPTAIN NAMAKA

QUAIL-GON

YODA BIRD

MOA WINDU

BLUE PADAWANS

MEET THE BIRD REBELS, JEDI BIRDS, AND THEIR FRIENDS!

CHUCK "HAM" SOLO

TEREBACCA

EWOK BIRDS

R2-EGG2

OBI-WAN KABOOMI

STELLA ORGANA

JAR JAR WINGS

C-3PYOLK

REDKIN SKYWALKER

RED SKYWALKER

Brave young Red Skywalker is a proud member of the Bird Rebels and a true hero. This feisty fowl is training to become a Jedi Bird—to help save the galaxy from an evil band of pigs!

FUN FACT
Fledgling Red is really clumsy. He keeps dropping his lightsaber and bumping into other birds.

Red is very proud of his gleaming blond feathers.

Blue lightsaber is poised to knock down pigs, objects, and buildings.

High flyer

This fast flyboy is the Bird Republic's bravest pilot. He has flown his X-wing Birdfighter all over the galaxy. He just needs to work on his clumsy landings!

Quick draw

Red has the best duelling teacher ever—Yoda Bird himself. A fast learner, Red can already draw his lightsaber quicker than you can say "pig." If only he could keep hold of it long enough to use it!

Brilliant bird bargain

Red buys droids R2-EGG2 and C-3PYOLK in a dodgy deal with a flock of Jawa Birds. Little does he know that R2-EGG2 is a disguise for The Egg...

DATA FILE

▶ **Home planet:**
Tatooine

▶ **Special skill:**
Lightsaber swipes

▶ **Bird buddy:**
Chuck "Ham" Solo

Red grew up in a humble desert hut on Tatooine.

DAGOBAH

The remote planet of Dagobah is full of dark forests, slimy swamps, and deadly creatures. Not many birds or pigs even know where to find Dagobah, so it's the perfect spot for Red to complete his Jedi training with Yoda in secret.

Slimy plants are draped all over Red's once-shiny X-wing Birdfighter.

PERHAPS A TOUR OF THE LAKE WASN'T SUCH A GOOD IDEA AFTER ALL...

Dragonsnake Bog is home to all kinds of weird egg-shaped blobs.

COMPLAINING ALREADY, ARE YOU? STUCK HERE FOR YEARS I HAVE BEEN.

Yoda's hideaway

Shrouded in clouds and in the middle of nowhere, Dagobah is the perfect planet for Yoda to stay on to hide from the Pork Side. It is a shame that swamp slugs are the only company!

R2-EGG2 stays put on the ship—he is afraid of swamp slugs!

R2-EGG2 is happy to assist when in Red's trusty X-wing fighter—but he is not impressed when Red crashes in one of Dagobah's swamps!

OBI-WAN KABOOMI

This wise Jedi Master is an explosive character. Kaboomi is a great teacher and has taught many young, angry Jedi Birds to control their Force powers. Sadly, however, he cannot always control his own!

His feathers may get ruffled, but Kaboomi's hairstyle is fully bombproof.

Kaboomi's eyebrows are heroic. He can use them to deflect small meteors.

Great Jedi

Kaboomi is a wise and highly skilled Jedi Bird Warrior, determined to protect The Egg at all costs. There's just one small problem—he has no idea where it is! Luckily for him, the pigs don't either.

BOMBASTIC JEDI MASTER

FUN FACT

Kaboomi trained both Redkin Skywalker and Red Skywalker in the Force.

Tough teacher

Kaboomi has to be patient when training his accident-prone pupil Red Skywalker. Of course, he knows what it is like to have a short fuse himself!

DATA FILE

▶ **Home planet:** Coruscant

▶ **Special skill:** Force blast

▶ **Bird buddies:** Chuck "Ham" Solo, Red Skywalker

Feel the Force

A Jedi should follow the path of peace, but Kaboomi secretly enjoys blasting things to bits. He aims to topple the Pig Empire, but anything else in his way is at risk, too.

WHAT DOES IT TAKE TO BE A GOOD JEDI BIRD?

Follow the path of peace—and avoid the temptations of the Pork Side.

Treat all life forms as equals—even pigs. They cannot all be bad, right?

Seek knowledge—especially knowledge of how to blow up the Pig Star.

Adventure. Excitement. Junk food. A Jedi Bird does not crave these things!

AN ANGRY BIRD,
A POWERFUL BIRD IS.
MASTER YOUR ANGER
YOU MUST!

CHUCK "HAM" SOLO

Chuck "Ham" Solo is a famous junk food smuggler. Despite mixing with some shifty criminals, Chuck is a hero who often lends a wing to help the Bird Rebels fight the pigs.

FUN FACT

When it comes to gambling, Chuck is a lucky bird. He won the *Mighty Falcon* ship in a game of cards.

Mixed-up Chuck

Confident Chuck considers himself one of the coolest guys in the galaxy, but he does not always look that way to others. In fact, it sometimes seems that this birdbrained adventurer has no clue what he is doing at all.

Handsome Ham loves grooming his plumage. Every feather is preened to a sheen.

Ever-ready Chuck rarely removes his holster.

COCKY BUT CONFUSED ADVENTURER

Love-struck Chuck

Chuck does only what he wants, so when Princess Stella orders him around it ruffles his feathers. He is left even more confused than usual when he finds himself falling in love with her.

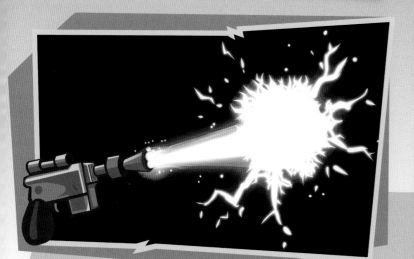

Ham's a blast!

Ham is a hotshot with his heavy blaster pistol. Its huge blast of firepower makes missing the target almost impossible!

DATA FILE

▶ **Home planet:** Corellia

▶ **Special skill:** Dodgy deals

▶ **Bird buddy:** Terebacca

TEREBACCA

This beast of a bird is Chuck "Ham" Solo's co-pilot and mechanic. Terebacca, or "Terry" as he is known to his friends, has a knack for fixing machines—he just thumps them. Nothing scares Terebacca, except maybe bath night.

Because of his thick, soft feathers, Terry looks cuddly for an angry bird.

Heavyweight hero

Terebacca is big enough to knock a planet out of orbit just by landing on it. Smuggling junk food does nothing to help Terry lose weight—he can't resist checking that all his goods are as tasty as they look!

One stare from Terry's beady eyes can turn a Pigtrooper into jelly!

FEARSOME FUZZBALL

Bird of few words

Terry is definitely the strong, silent type. His language sounds just like tweets and grunts to the other birds. Only best buddy Chuck Solo can understand him.

DATA FILE

▶ **Home planet:**
Kashyyyk

▶ **Special skill:**
Being humungous

▶ **Bird buddy:**
Chuck "Ham" Solo

Fast friends

Smuggling is a risky business, and danger follows Terebacca and Chuck wherever they go. Luckily their trusty (and rusty) ship, the *Mighty Falcon*, is fast enough to outrun any Imperial starship.

MIGHTY FALCON

It may not look like the fastest ship in the galaxy, but this freighter has been souped-up by Chuck "Ham" Solo. Now it has hidden surprises, with a light-speed warp drive and more gadgets than a pig can shake a stick at.

FUN FACT

Although fast, the *Falcon* is unreliable, and is famous for breaking down when you least expect it!

Heat exhaust vents keep the ship cool.

SUPER SMUGGLING STARSHIP

Great ship

The pigs are always fooled by the *Falcon*'s looks. It may appear to be a hunk of junk, but it is faster than a Pigtrooper after a free Jogan fruit cake. When it jumps to light speed it can outrun any ship in the Pig Empire.

This radar dish alerts the Bird Rebels to incoming Pig TIE fighters.

The secret compartments are great places to hide from Pigtroopers.

Hidden missiles for firing at those silly swines!

Quick escape

For a fast getaway, this ship has been known to try the ol' slingshot maneuver—with a real slingshot!

Chuck and Terebacca pilot the ship from the egg-shaped cockpit.

Previous owner

Once owned by Lando Birdissian, the *Falcon* was won by Chuck in a game of snap. The old friends are still fighting over who truly deserves to have it.

RED SKYWALKER

FIGHTS FOR:
Jedi and the Bird Rebels

STRENGTHS:
Red is a whizz with a lightsaber and is able to use the Force for spectacular leaps during fast-paced duels!

WEAKNESSES:
Take cover! Red's lightsaber does not always quite hit the target—especially when he sees red and becomes really angry.

LARD VADER

FIGHTS FOR:
The Pig Empire (and for himself!)

STRENGTHS:
Lard is a fiendish master of the Force and can send his bird enemies flying through the air.

WEAKNESSES:
Lard Vader is not as fit or as quick as he used to be. Too much junk food and having his porky minions do everything for him has made him slow!

PRINCESS STELLA ORGANA

As one of the Bird Republic's leaders, Stella Organa is a bird on a mission. The plucky princess means to overthrow the Pig Empire, which wants to rule the entire galaxy. Those pigs will soon be trembling with fear!

The Princess is one bold bird. She takes no nonsense from bird or pig!

Fight path

Stella might be a beautiful princess, but if she has to get her claws dirty she won't be upset. In fact, Stella is usually first in line for a fight, especially with the Pork Empire.

Stella wears her hair in two braided coils. Feather cuts are not her style!

THE REBELLIOUS ROYAL

FUN FACT
Eagle-eyed and steady of wing, the princess is a very good shot with a weapon and always hits her target.

Bossy bird
Stubborn Stella is used to getting her own way. The daring and determined princess expects everybody to obey her orders. Immediately!

Gravitational Field Disruptor
The princess's favorite weapon is the Gravitational Field Disruptor. With it, she can adjust the weight of any object and then fling it at her piggy foes.

DATA FILE
▶ **Home planet:**
Alderaan

▶ **Special skill:**
Sharp shooter

▶ **Bird buddy:**
Chuck "Ham" Solo

WHAT DOES IT TAKE TO BE A SMUGGLER?

Don't be nosey— never ask questions about the cargo you are carrying.

A GOOD SMUGGLER HAS TO BE BRAVE, TOUGH, HANDSOME, AND VERY LUCKY-LIKE ME.

Make some powerful friends—and try not to be put on Jabba's hitlist.

Find yourself a hefty sidekick—tough fuzzball friends can come in handy!

Learn to be a sharp shooter with a blaster—you never know who might be on your tail.

REDKIN SKYWALKER

Redkin Skywalker is no birdbrain and has more Force power than any other bird. Jedi Bird Quail-Gon believes Redkin is the Chosen One, able to save the galaxy from the evil pigs. Redkin fears nothing—except maybe asking young queen Peckmé Amidala on a date (what if she says no?).

Rumor has it that Redkin uses the Force to style his spiky hair.

Angry Jedi

Redkin Skywalker makes pigtroopers squeal with fear, while other Jedi Birds admire his bravery. There is just one problem—this bird loses his temper very easily and a Jedi must always remain calm in the face of danger!

FUN FACT

Brilliant at building machines, Redkin Skywalker built the droid C-3PYOLK—all out of spare parts!

Patient master

Redkin's teacher, Obi-Wan Kaboomi, guides him wisely, but cannot help noticing his Padawan's fondness for extra fries with everything! Could this lead Redkin to the Pork Side?

Champion chick Podracer

Podracing is seen as a dangerous waste of time by some! Not by Redkin. He won a big race on Tatooine—freeing him from slavery!

DATA FILE

▶ **Home planet:**
Tatooine

▶ **Special skills:**
Force power,
Ace mechanic,
Podracing pilot

▶ **Bird buddy:**
Obi-Wan Kaboomi

C-3PYOLK

Unlike his Bird Rebel masters, C-3PYOLK is never angry. This golden droid bird is specially programmed to keep the peace. He speaks many languages—all of them politely.

Born worried

C-3PYOLK is easily scared. In fact he is bit of a chicken! The distressed droid tends to flap at the first sign of trouble—and there is always a lot of trouble when you are fighting the Pork Federation!

C-3PYOLK likes to stay dazzlingly shiny. His metal plumage is as polished as his manners.

This diligent droid makes sure his nuts and bolts are fastened tight.

NERVY REBEL ROBOT

DATA FILE
▶ **Droid type:**
Protocol

▶ **Special skill:**
Translation

▶ **Droid dude:**
R2-EGG2

Cracking up!
When C-3PYOLK is under attack he often goes to pieces—quite literally! He can look as though he is in trouble, but his sharp jagged edges actually help to repel the enemy.

Great escape
C-3PYOLK gives the Pork Side the slip in a tiny escape pod heading toward Tatooine. Luckily, brave buddy R2-EGG2 is by his side to make the flight seem less of a fright.

REDKIN SKYWALKER

FIGHTS FOR:
The Bird Rebels. At least, for now...

STRENGTHS:
Redkin is a very angry bird. When he sees red he loses all sense of fear and flies into a fighting frenzy that few birds can match!

WEAKNESSES:
Mixed-up Redkin is not quite sure which side he is on. That is a bit of a problem in a duel!

COUNT DODO

FIGHTS FOR:
The Pork Side

STRENGTHS:
This ex-Jedi Bird Warrior has had more duels than most pigs have had junk food dinners. Nobody has more experience than the Count.

WEAKNESSES:
Count Dodo has been around a long time and is slightly past his prime. He still has the skills, but does he have the energy?

R2-EGG2

R2-EGG2 is a devoted droid servant to the Jedi Birds. He can act a bit shell-shocked at times, but the birds know that this trusty little droid will never let them down.

Talkative R2 loves arguing with his droid pal C-3PYOLK.

Eggstreme secret

The egg-shaped droid looks harmless enough, but he is hiding a big secret. Nestled within him is The Egg, which contains the Force. Both the Jedi Birds and the Sith Lards are seeking its amazing power.

R2-EGG2 sometimes goes into a sulk and switches himself off.

LITTLE DROID WITH A BIG SECRET

Yoda knows all

Years ago, Yoda Bird hid The Egg in R2-EGG2 to keep it safe, but he forgot to tell anybody. Will he ever remember?

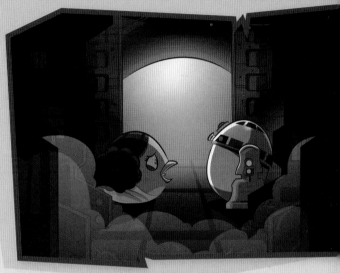

Recording service

R2 is great for recording messages on. When Princess Stella is caught by Lard Vader, she records a distress call on R2 to send to Obi-Wan.

Shock-arm power

In battle, R2 is more hard-boiled than he looks. His shock arm delivers a jolt of electricity that blasts through piggy defenses with ease.

DATA FILE

▷ **Built by:**
Yoda Bird

▷ **Special skill:**
Egg hiding

▷ **Droid dude:**
C-3PYOLK

37

WHAT DOES IT TAKE TO BE A GOOD DROID BIRD?

Keep yourself in eggs-ellent shape—take two oil baths every day.

Act scared all the time—it makes your Jedi Bird companions look even braver!

It is your duty as a droid to avoid getting damaged—always let someone else face the danger first!

You need good language skills. In a galactic war it is good to be able to cry for help in six million different languages.

DROIDS MUST ALWAYS BE POLITE—NEVER TELL A JEDI JUST HOW CRAZY THE PLANS THEY HAVE HATCHED REALLY ARE!

YODA BIRD

Yoda is a respected Jedi Bird Master and one of the wisest beings in the galaxy. But thinking deeply for centuries is hard work and the green genius can be a bit absent-minded!

FUN FACT

Nobody knows which planet Yoda was hatched on, or even what type of bird he is!

Bird with a secret

Only Yoda knows the secret of where The Egg is—inside R2-EGG2! Yoda wants to get cracking and break the news to Red Skywalker. He does not believe, however, that Red is ready to learn the truth.

Aging Yoda has been almost bald for several centuries.

Yoda always wears the same homespun robes—and they could use a wash!

LEGENDARY WISE OLD BIRD

DATA FILE

▶ Adopted planet:
Dagobah

▶ Special skills:
Wisdom, lightsaber

▶ Bird buddy:
Red Skywalker

Feathered Force

When it comes to combat, Yoda is lightning-quick with a lightsaber! He uses the full might of the Force to leap around and outwit his opponents. Then he strikes them with a winning blow.

Ready, Jedi, Go!

When Yoda trains Red to be a Jedi on the gloomy swamps of the planet Dagobah, he proves to be a tough teacher, pushing the rookie rebel to his very limit.

THE ART OF THE LIGHTSABER

The lightsaber is the favorite weapon of the
Jedi Birds. A controlled beam of plasma
energy powered by a special crystal,
it can slice through almost anything.
The bad news for Jedi Birds is that
the bad guys have got them too!

> A JEDI USES HIS
> LIGHTSABER ONLY IN
> SELF-DEFENSE, OR TO SLICE
> UP PIGGY STUFF!

Skywalker skill

Some lucky Jedi Birds are
born with special Force
powers that make them
naturally expert with the lightsaber.
Red can even use one with his eyes
closed! Red has a pale-blue lightsaber,
like many Jedi. The bad guys prefer red.

Pork Side duels

Even Red has trouble dueling with Lard Vader, whose lightsaber skills are hard to match. Plus Vader has a height advantage (he stands on his pig minions), so he is able to tower over his bird rivals!

Ready stance

Jedi Birds are taught to stand in a special way in preparation for a lightsaber duel. A calm pose helps them to feel the Force. It also helps them to look cool.

Greedy Grunter

Darth Moar may fight with two blades, but greedy General Grunter likes to have four! He uses lightsabers that he has stolen from his foes because he is too lazy to make his own!

> **FOUR BLADES ARE BETTER THAN ONE! NO WONDER MY ENEMIES GO TO PIECES!**

43

TATOOINE

In the Outer Rim of the galaxy is a desert world that appears quite peaceful from a distance, but it is really a hangout for smugglers, gangsters, and Jedi! It is famous for its twin suns, Jabba the Hog's palace, and also for being the home of young Red Skywalker.

Mess Eisley is the spaceport of this far-flung world. Its cantina is famous throughout the galaxy—for its fights!

This device detects hazards like sandstorms—and Jabba's burps.

RED IS STRONG WITH THE FORCE. WE COULD KICK SOME PORK TOGETHER!

WHEN R2-EGG2 AND C-3PYOLK ARRIVED, I KNEW IT WAS TIME FOR ME TO FLY THE NEST.

Red's homeworld

Red Skywalker may be a Jedi Bird now, but he grew up on a humble moisture farm on Tatooine. While he was buying droids for the farm he met R2-EGG2 and C-3PYOLK—and his life was never the same again!

Buildings have piggy faces to frighten away the local Sand People.

BLUE PADAWANS
AWESOME APPRENTICES

These crazy chicks are apprentice Jedi Birds. They aim to have lots of fun before they become full-fledged Jedi, so they can be a bit reckless. The enthusiastic Padawans are trained by Jedi Master Yoda.

FUN FACT
Beware these plucky little learners—in battle they can join together and fight as one mighty, feathered force!

Novice helmets protect Padawans during frequent food fights.

Blue battlers
The Padawans must listen to Yoda's orders—even when they have no intention of following them! But being unpredictable in battle comes in very handy when facing the Pork Side—the pigs never know what to expect.

All young trainees have the short Padawan haircut.

CAPTAIN NAMAKA
SECURITY SUPREMO

Head of security on Planet Naboo, Captain Namaka is devoted to keeping Peckmé Amidala safe. Namaka has a superfast reaction time of almost zero, which means no Pigtrooper ever beats him to the draw.

Many jealous foes have tried to steal Namaka's splendid hat.

Royal protector
This suspicious security expert sees danger everywhere. Namaka will not hesitate to use his blaster to blow away any threat to Peckmé.

DATA FILE

▷ **Home planet:**
Naboo

▷ **Special skill:**
Bird bodyguard

▷ **Bird buddy:**
Peckmé Amidala

47

WHAT DOES IT TAKE TO BE AN ACE X-WING PILOT?

Practice high-speed maneuvers— even though pig TIE fighters are lousy shots.

Use your torpedoes wisely! They don't grow on trees, you know!

Be careful where you park your Birdfighter— try not to get it ticketed.

ONE BIRDFIGHTER MAY BE SMALL, BUT TOGETHER WE CAN DESTROY THE PIG STAR...WE HOPE!

Always listen to your droid co-pilot—even when you can't unscramble what it is saying!

MOA WINDU

This serious Jedi is feared and respected by birds and pigs alike. He has a suspicious nature and has mastered the art of the Jedi frown, which can transmit a bad mood throughout the entire galaxy.

Moa may lack feathers on his head, but he makes up for it in style.

Moa always wears his trusty utility belt and the standard brown Jedi tunic.

Cool character

Moa is the envy of all the other Jedi who try to copy his cool image. He never cracks a smile in victory, nor has his feathers ruffled in defeat.

FUN FACT

Moa Windu may not be able to fly, but he loves fighting and floating in the zero gravity of space!

Lightsaber ace

Moa's violet blade is unique and is powered by a rare purple jewel. He is one of the greatest lightsaber masters, having been trained by the great Yoda Bird.

DATA FILE

▶ **Home planet:**
Haruun Kool

▶ **Special skill:**
Lightsaber combat

▶ **Bird buddies:**
Yoda, Obi-Wan

Jedi High Council

Moa is a member of the Jedi High Council, second only to Yoda in the pecking order. He often explains Yoda's orders to the others if the Jedi leader jumbles up his sentences too much.

Jar Jar Wings
Long-Tongued Naboo Senator

Jar Jar Wings might look a little goofy and act a little strange, but this bird is no yolk! He is a Senator for the planet of Naboo and a General—he isn't afraid to battle alongside his Jedi buddies to defeat the Pork Side.

Data File

▷ Home planet: Naboo

▷ Special skill: Tongue swing

▷ Bird buddies: Peckmé Amidala, Quail-Gon

Jar Jar's long scaly ears help keep him airborne.

Tasty target
Jar Jar's googly eyes on stalks help him spot treats from high up in the sky, and his big beak is great for scooping up candy. It's a shame this clumsy fowl often drops it all before he can gobble it!

PECKMÉ AMIDALA
NABOO'S COURAGEOUS QUEEN

As the Queen of Naboo, Peckmé Amidala appears serene and calm. But don't be fooled! With pigs invading her planet, Peckmé is one exceptionally angry bird and is ready for a fight!

DATA FILE

▶ Home planet:
Naboo

▶ Special skill:
Gravity pull

▶ Bird buddies:
Redkin Skywalker, Jar Jar Wings

Shake and quake

Peckmé proves she is more than a match for the Pork Side. She can use her power to pull gravity, causing the ground to shake and her enemies to quake in fear!

Peckmé raises her royal eyebrow when she feels haughty.

Long eyelashes for fluttering her way out of trouble.

DARTH SWINDLE

FIGHTS FOR:
The Pork Side

STRENGTHS:
This Pig Lord is a dangerous duelist. He has great powers of persuasion, which he uses to convince others like Redkin to help him.

WEAKNESSES:
Whoops! Piglatine's Force lightning bolts can be reflected by an opponent's lightsaber and sent right back at him.

MOA WINDU

FIGHTS FOR:
The Jedi Birds

STRENGTHS:
Stunning skills and fast footwork make Moa one of the best lightsaber fighters around. Windu usually wins!

WEAKNESSES:
Moa's biggest weakness is that he cannot fly. However, this is less of a problem than not being able to trust friends such as Redkin.

WHAT DOES IT TAKE TO BE A BIRD REBEL PRINCESS?

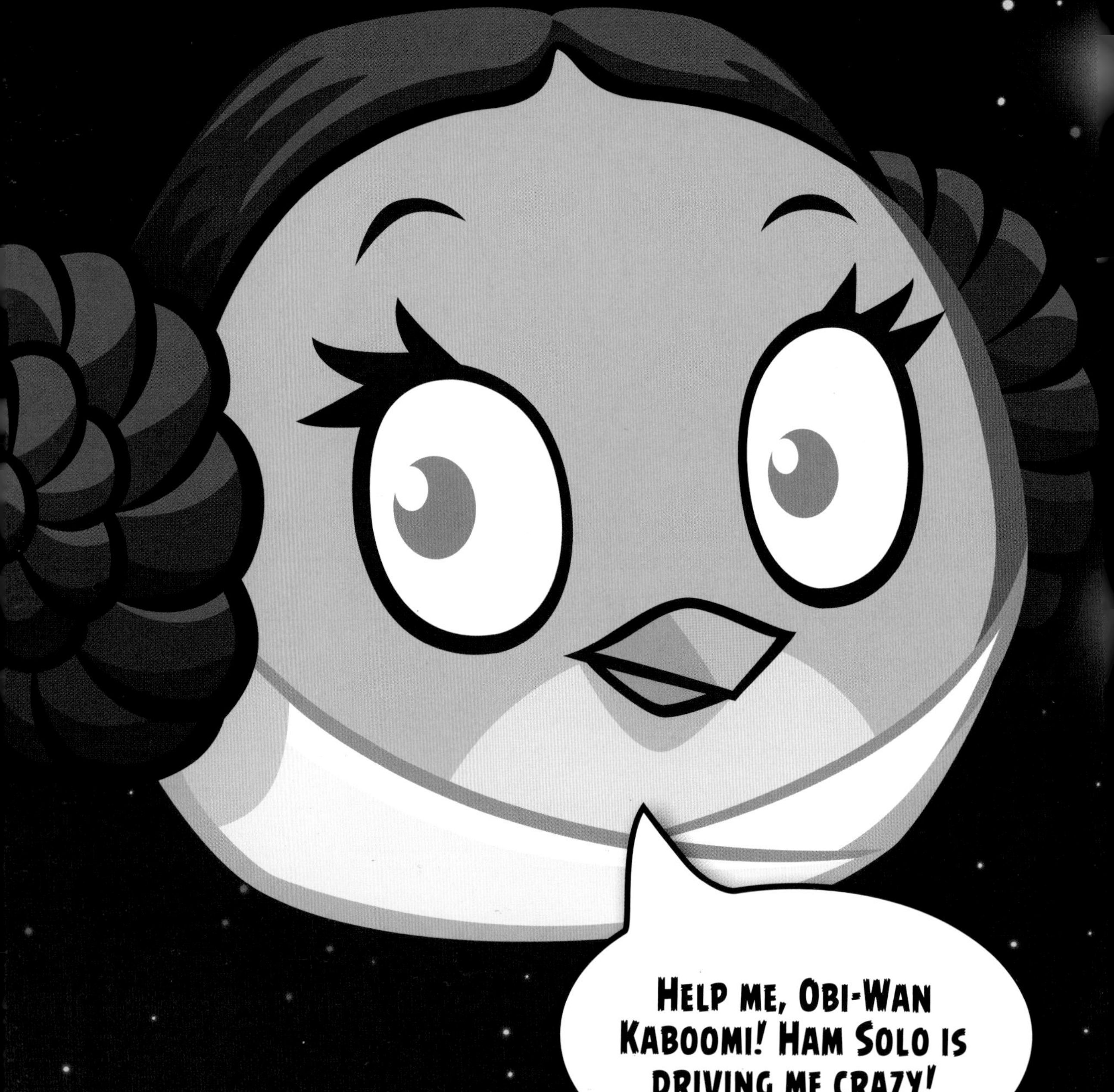

Surround yourself with brave heroes—then show them what you are made of!

Do not admit to any other birds that you like them—especially Ham Solo!

Squawk loudly. This ensures every rebel knows which bird is in charge.

You need good hair—a unique hairstyle always gets you noticed.

BEST BIRD BUDDIES

Among the birds there are some firm friendships. Some have known each other for years, while others are just starting out. They say birds of a feather stick together, and that certainly seems to be true for this flock!

Chuck "Ham" Solo and Terry

These chirpy pals have a deep understanding... Ham is the only bird who understands what Terry is saying!

R2-EGG2 and C-3PYOLK

This droid double-act goes everywhere together. They always help (and sometimes even mend) each other.

Obi-Wan and Quail-Gon

Jedi Bird Quail-Gon takes Obi-Wan under his wing as his mentor, but they also enjoy each other's company.

Redkin and Peckmé

These young birds like each other a lot. Even though it is not allowed, a royal romance starts to develop!

When you're being attacked, you find out who your true friends are. Being close pals helps the Bird Rebels pull together as one so they can fight the Pork Side!

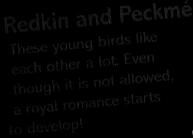

QUEEN PECKMÉ AMIDALA

LIKES:

Peace. Peckmé simply hates war—and she is prepared to blast anyone who disagrees with her!

Redkin Skywalker. The Queen truly believes she can bring out his good side.

HATES:

Count Dodo—for stirring up trouble and leading a junk food uprising.

Always being in danger. Invasions and bungled kidnappings become boring after a while!

I DON'T WANT A WAR, BUT THOSE PESKY PIGS ARE JUST MAKING ME SO ANGRY!

Princess Stella Organa

LIKES:

Being a rebel. She hates being told what to do by the Pig Empire!

Chuck "Ham" Solo—though she hates to admit it. The sneaky smuggler is big-headed enough already!

HATES:

The Pig Star. It must be blown to bits—and hopefully all the bad guys with it, in a pig hog roast!

Chuck ignoring her orders. When you are a princess everyone really ought to do what you say!

SOME BIRDS ACCUSE ME OF BEING A BOSSY BOOTS. BUT SOMEBODY HAS TO BE IN CHARGE, RIGHT?

THE CITY OF THEED

Theed is the capital city of the planet Naboo. The good news is that it's spectacularly beautiful, has a rich history, and is home to the Royal Palace. The bad news is it is now occupied by the Pork Side!

LET'S GET CRACKING AND SAVE THIS CITY'S BACON FROM THE PORK SIDE!

SEE WHAT THEY HAVE DONE TO THIS PLACE? IT LOOKS LIKE A PIGSTY!

Peckmé's palace

With Theed Palace now full of porkers, brave Peckmé and her security birds break back into her old home. Can she pull off an amazing rescue and throw out the pigs?

The shape of this grand arch in Theed Palace clearly resembles Peckmé's eyebrows.

The beautifully constructed columns in the palace are enormous.

Theed Palace is full of gigantic columns, elegant arches, and statues of royal ancestors. It took a long time to build!

63

QUAIL-GON

This bold Jedi Bird likes to do things his way. Quail-Gon is never happy to go along with the flock—even Yoda Bird has trouble telling him what to do! This is why he will never sit on the Jedi High Council...

Quail ties back his long hair, so he can see during battles.

Headstrong Jedi

Quail-Gon takes on missions that would make other Jedi quiver and quail. He even met Lard Vader when Vader was young and saw great power in him— not realizing what a menace he would turn out to be!

His long Jedi robe and tunic are great for swishing around in.

REBELLIOUS JEDI WARRIOR

FUN FACT

The evil Count Dodo was Quail-Gon's teacher, before Dodo went over to the Pork Side!

Sith showdown

Even though Quail-Gon is a great warrior, he was shocked when he fought Darth Moar —the Jedi thought the Sith were extinct! Quail-Gon certainly wished Darth Moar was.

Kaboomi's teacher

Although usually grumpy, Quail-Gon showed great patience training Obi-Wan Kaboomi. He was even blown up by him a couple of times before his Padawan learned to have better control over his powers.

DATA FILE

▶ Home planet: Unknown

▶ Special skill: Feeling the Force

▶ Bird buddy: Obi-Wan Kaboomi

HOTH

The remote and lonely planet of Hoth is covered in frozen wastelands of snow and ice. Because nobody ever goes there, this very cold planet is a very cool place to build a secret Bird Rebel base.

Each mechanical AT-AT Walker is controlled by a Pigtrooper.

The powerful grips ensure the giant machines do not slip on the ice and snow.

AWAARWWWGGGG!
WAARGH!
AWAARWWWGGGG!

I SAID, "IT IS ICY ON HOTH" NOT "IT IS NICE AND HOT!"

Echo Base

Echo Base is the rebels' secret HQ. This vast cave complex carved into the mountains makes any sound echo—including Ham Solo and Princess Stella's arguing!

Snow collects in massive drifts on icy Hoth.

Lard Vader invades Hoth when he discovers the rebels' base. A bitter battle rages involving huge snow walkers!

LANDO BIRDISSIAN

Smooth-squawking Lando Birdissian just oozes charm, and he puts it to good use—making himself rich! He is a suave smuggler and one of the greatest gamblers in the galaxy.

Feathered friend

Lando might be a silver-beaked charmer, but he has a heart of gold. After first betraying the Bird Rebels, conscience-stricken Lando returns to help them give the Pork Side a good roasting.

Lookin' good! This bird's mustache and eyebrows are always neatly groomed.

Lando's robes are made from the finest materials money can buy.

FUN FACT

One of Lando's biggest ever gambling wins was Cloud City, a mining colony on the planet Bespin.

Ham sandwiched!

Under pressure from Lard Vader, Lando betrays his pal Chuck Solo to the Pork Side. Lando feels awful when he sees Ham encased in carbonite!

Cloud City administrator

As Baron Administrator of Cloud City, Lando is responsible for keeping the city safe. This important position allows him to show off his talents—and his flashy robes!

DATA FILE

▶ **Home planet:**
Unknown

▶ **Special skill:**
Smooth talking

▶ **Bird buddy:**
Chuck "Ham" Solo

69

From EAGER PADAWAN to EVIL PORKER

1 Podracer Redkin

Young Redkin is a racing ace and even built his own Podracer. When it comes to speed, Redkin is keen and eager to succeed!

2 Padawan Redkin

Determined Redkin is ready to be a Jedi and starts his training with Obi-Wan Kaboomi. As a rising star, he gets off to a flying start!

THIS BIRD WILL BECOME A JEDI KNIGHT. HE IS A HIGH FLIER!

FOCUS YOUR ATTENTION ON TRAINING, NOT JUST ME, REDKIN!

Evil Redkin?

As Redkin grows up, he becomes more confused and angry! The bitter bird starts to wonder if he should fight for the Pork Side.

Lard Vader

In the end, Redkin Skywalker becomes an evil porker! As vile Lard Vader, this Jedi Bird's journey to the Pork Side is complete.

EWOK BIRDS
FLUFFY FLIERS

Ewok Birds are both friendly and fluffy-feathered. These cuddly creatures fly in large flocks all over the galaxy, cheerfully chirping away. Unfortunately, nobody knows what they are going on about!

DATA FILE
▶ Home planet:
Endor
▶ Special skills:
Loud singing, using catapults
▶ Bird buddies:
Any Bird Rebel

Ewok Birds always dress in simple brown robes, complete with furry ears!

Excitable Ewoks

Ewok Birds squawk louder and louder when they are excited! Their tweets are noisiest when they meet Bird Rebels. In fact, your hearing could be damaged by their ear-splitting screeches!

BLUE SQUADRON
PILOT BIRDS

Blue Squadron birds always fly in a formation of one, and then split into three to confuse the enemy! Each tremendous trio of these reliable and brave Bird Rebels is dedicated to fighting the Pork Side!

The very famous squadron helmet, worn with pride.

The orange line helps the birds see each other.

FUN FACT
It takes many years of training to become a member of Blue Squadron. And of course you need to be blue!

Flying colors
Many birds want to wear the prestigious blue-and-white helmets of the Blue Squadron. In fact, these crack pilots make many other birds turn green with envy!

WELCOME TO THE PORK SIDE

PORK SIDE LINE-UP

LARD VADER

PIGTROOPER

DARTH SWINDLE

JANGO FATT

PIG STAR TROOPER

JAWA BIRD

MYNHOGS

DARTH MOAR

AT-AT PILOT

GENERAL GRUNTER

TIE FIGHTER PILOT

TUSKEN RAIDER

MEET THE VILLAINS OF THE PORK SIDE AND THEIR EVIL SUPPORTERS!

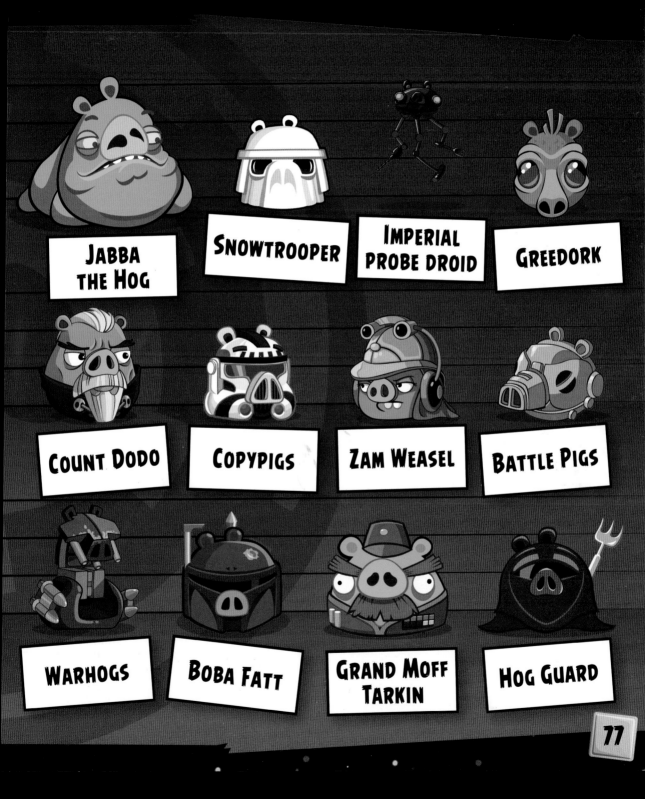

JABBA THE HOG

SNOWTROOPER

IMPERIAL PROBE DROID

GREEDORK

COUNT DODO

COPYPIGS

ZAM WEASEL

BATTLE PIGS

WARHOGS

BOBA FATT

GRAND MOFF TARKIN

HOG GUARD

LARD VADER

Evil Lard Vader is the most power-hungry military commander in the galaxy. The Pig Empire leader is desperate to unscramble the mystery of The Egg. It could help him to achieve his ultimate goal—becoming emperor!

Mask of mystery

Millions of piggy minions look up to Lard Vader. They don't know that the Pork Side commander has a fowl secret—he is actually a bird! In fact he used to be one of the Jedi before he switched sides.

Hard helmet protects him from strikes by oncoming birds.

Mask covers Lard Vader's beak and helps him to breathe—very, very loudly.

Evil Lord of the Pork

Low-down Lard Vader

The Pork Side leader is short-tempered, short in patience, and short in stature, too. Under his robes he stands on a pair of pigs to make himself look taller.

Princess prisoner

Lard Vader captures Princess Stella. He grills her for information about The Egg, but she doesn't crack under the pressure.

Fun Fact

Vader's helmet and suit is his life-support machine. He cannot breathe without it.

Data File

▶ **Home planet:**
Tatooine

▶ **Special skill:**
Being thoroughly evil

▶ **Pig pals:**
None: Everyone is an enemy

Lard Vader flew this new, advanced fighter aircraft as he tried to defend the Pig Star. Although faster than the standard TIE fighter, it was still too slow for Ham Solo's *Mighty Falcon*!

TIE terror
Vader wanted his fighter to look like him, so he could scare his enemies from afar!

Twin viewing window

Laser blaster cannon

Vader's extras
Larger, heavier, and with bigger fridge-space than the standard TIE fighter, Vader's advanced model has a private bathroom for longer flights.

Special bracket-shaped wings make a cool sound

STANDARD
TIE FIGHTER

This menacing machine is one of the most feared in all of space, even among the pig army! It has no shields and no life-support systems—piggy pilots have to wear space suits and hope for the best!

FUN FACT
TIE fighters patrol in large groups—the pilots are not clever enough to think on their own.

Solar wings power the twin engines

Sensor snout detects Jedi birdfighters

Perfect pilots?
Only the very worst pig pilots are chosen to fly TIE fighters. The swines have to be stupendously stupid to climb into one of these flying targets!

81

DARTH MOAR

FIGHTS FOR:
The Pork Side

STRENGTHS:
Darth Moar is very dangerous with his double-bladed lightsaber. Attacking with both blades means double trouble for his enemies.

WEAKNESSES:
Junk-food obsessed Moar can get easily distracted during a duel by the thought of a tasty snack!

Obi-Wan Kaboomi

Fights for:
The Jedi Birds

Strengths:
When it comes to the Force, Obi-Wan is number one! This power can really give him a big advantage over Darth Moar.

Weaknesses:
Obi-Wan Kaboomi's explosive nature means that he might detonate during a fight when he does not mean to!

JANGO FATT

This battling bounty hunter is a weapons expert. Jango Fatt was raised by a gang of fierce Hamdalorian warriors. He will happily hunt down birds for a fee—of a triple-thick swill shake—and is one of the most feared fighters in the galaxy.

This jetpack helps Jango to shoot off from the scene of his crimes.

Cloned pig

Jango Fatt was cloned by the Empire, and now there are thousands of Copypigs who share his piggy physique. Luckily for everyone else, Jango mostly keeps himself hidden under a hi-tech helmet.

The visor on Jango's helmet allows him to see what is behind him.

WEAPONS MASTER

FUN FACT
When Jango was cloned, he asked to keep one of the clones for himself—and brought him up as his own spoiled son, Boba Fatt!

Dastardly dad
Jango likes to set a bad example to his son, Boba. They both compete to be the meanest member of the family.

Jango's blaster
Jango always carries lots of weapons, and if he ever remembers where he has put them, the galaxy is in trouble! His blaster gun is his most treasured possession.

DATA FILE
▶ Home planet:
Concord Dawn

▶ Special skill:
Gadget guru

▶ Awful ally:
Count Dodo

PIGTROOPERS
MINDLESS MARAUDERS

These porky pilferers rampage across the galaxy, sniffing out junk food and bringing it back to Piglatine. They wear white armor, which makes them easy to spot—and to destroy!

FUN FACT

Pigtroopers used to be Copypigs working for the Bird Rebels. But junk food lured them over to the Pork Side.

Silly soldiers

This blundering band of soldiers is trained to follow orders without question. Pigtroopers have no ideas of their own. They are easy to take by surprise and when on a mission, generally prefer to snack than attack!

Earpiece picks up orders that they do not completely understand.

Cheap armor offers no real protection in battle.

SNOWTROOPERS
FROZEN TASKFORCE

Sent to snowy planets in icy conditions, this squad usually has no idea where they are or what they are doing! They are more expert at building snowpigs and glugging hot chocolate than fighting.

Helmet can be used as soup bowl at chow time.

Chilled pork

Every Snowtrooper is given a specially heated suit to survive in cold weather, but they have no idea how to turn it on, so they freeze anyway!

FUN FACT

Polarized goggles come in useful as Snowtroopers can nap on duty and no-one can see their eyes are shut!

87

CLOUD CITY

The planet Bespin's gas-mining colony seems like the perfect place for the Bird Rebels to hide from the Pork Side. This floating city is home to luxury hotels and casinos reserved for the very richest of birds!

The *Mighty Falcon* is ready and waiting if the birds need to make a swift escape.

Discovered!

When Lard Vader is tipped off that the Bird Rebels are in Cloud City, Pork Side forces arrive to snout around and hunt down Ham and Stella. The Pigtroopers soon take them prisoner.

This landing pad usually caters for craft full of tourists.

The view from a room in Cloud City is amazing!

OF COURSE I WON'T TELL LARD VADER THAT YOU ARE HERE!

The Bird Rebels think that they are safe in Cloud City, but governor Lando Birdissian's promise to protect them proves to be hot air!

DARTH SWINDLE

As well as being a Sith Lard, dastardly Darth Swindle is the evil leader of the Pig Empire who goes by the name of Piglatine. With his face always hidden by his hood, Swindle is as mysterious as he is dangerous!

A handy place for Swindle to hide his favorite fork.

Swindling swine

For years, Darth Swindle told the biggest porky ever! Everyone thought he was respectable Emperor Piglatine, but the cloaked con artist covered up his real identity as double-crossing Darth Swindle.

Swindle's large snout is always sticking out from beneath his hood.

DATA FILE

▶ **Home planet:**
Naboo

▶ **Special skill:**
Sith lightning

▶ **Pig pals:**
Lard Vader

Force lightning

Swindle uses the energy of the Force to increase his piggy powers. His most feared weapon is lethal Sith lightning that he shoots from the tips of his hooves!

FUN FACT

Swindle has banned junk food just so the greedy pig can keep it all for himself!

Bad influence

Emperors are meant to set a good example, but not Darth Swindle. The thoroughly rotten porker helps persuade Redkin Skywalker to turn to the Pork Side.

JABBA THE HOG

A greedy crime boss, Jabba has put on weight by buying, selling, and eating junk food. He thinks that he's running an important takeout service—by *taking* food from anyone who isn't Jabba the Hog!

Thick skin oozes stinky slime that can be used as oil for cooking junk food.

Pork palace

Jabba doesn't need to hide away like most criminals—he's so powerful he lives like a king in a palace. There he is surrounded by bodyguards, slaves, and a 24/7 all-you-can-eat buffet. Friends eat from the buffet, enemies may end up as a plate on it!

Jabba's body has no skeleton—much like a slug's.

JUNK FOOD LORD

Princess prisoner

This fearless flab-heap is quite happy to hold a princess prisoner if he can make a profit from it. He loves feeding captives to his pet monster, the Lardsack, the only thing hungrier than him!

> **MAYBE I SHOULD TURN CHUCK "HAM" SOLO INTO A "HAM" SANDWICH!**

FUN FACT

Jabba operates behind Lard Vader's back and hires junk food smugglers like Chuck Solo to do his bidding.

DATA FILE

▶ **Home planet:** Nal Hutta

▶ **Special skill:** Epic eating

▶ **Bad buddies:** Boba Fatt, Greedork

Jabba's buddy

Jabba likes hanging out with Greedork, a bounty hunter who will do anything for treats. The Hog likes having Greedork around—he is so weird-looking, that he makes Jabba look handsome!

IMPERIAL PROBE DROID
PORK SIDE PROBE PESTS

Imperial probe droids are a right royal pain! These sneaky, secret mechanical menaces have been programmed by the Pork Side to fly around the galaxy in search of the Bird Rebels' hideouts.

Perfectly designed beady eyes search for Bird Rebels!

Dangerous droids

When an Imperial probe droid finds a Bird Rebel base, it sends back pictures and other data to the Pork Side. One particularly pesky probe discovered the rebels' Echo Base headquarters on the planet Hoth!

FUN FACT

If an Imperial probe droid is captured, it can self-destruct!

Special tools help droids gain access to hidden entrances.

PIG STAR TROOPER
ELITE PORKY FORCES

Pig Star troopers are an elite band of specially selected Pork Side soldiers who carry out a variety of important duties. These prime porkers protect the Pig Star and operate its most deadly weapons.

Pig Star life

On the Pig Star, the troopers have comfortable quarters. There is even a canteen serving their favorite junk foods!

Super troopers

The troopers are fiercely loyal to Lard Vader and the Pork Side. These pigs know that if anything goes wrong with the Pig Star they will get a roasting!

Pig Star troopers always wear a smart, dark uniform.

WHAT MAKES A GOOD BIRD TURN BAD?

I WAS A GOOD JEDI UNTIL I TASTED THE PORK SIDE. AND I'VE PUT ON WEIGHT, TOO!

Scowling, stomping off, and not eating your vegetables is a sure path to the Pork Side.

Too much anger—even for an angry bird—is a dangerous thing. Stay cool!

Not following the rules of the Jedi Order will end in disaster! Listen to your Jedi Master.

Anger, resentment, arrogance? All great attributes—if you are a Sith Lard or evil pig!

AT-AT WALKER PILOT
PIGS ON STILTS

Piloting an AT-AT Walker isn't easy. In fact you need a good sense of direction, excellent battle skills, and loyalty to the Pork Side. And the rigorous training needed isn't a walk in the park either!

Skating on ice

The pigs use AT-ATs in tough battles on the icy wastelands of Hoth. Watch out for frostbite in those hooves!

Don't look down

If you're scared of heights, don't become an AT-AT pilot! Each Pigtrooper sits very high above the ground, steering the giant into battle and trying not to slip.

Reinforced helmet in case a pilot takes a tumble.

TIE FIGHTER PILOT
FEARLESS AVIATOR PIG

Depending on whether you're a bird or a pig, TIE fighter pilots are the bravest or stupidest pigs on the Pork Side. These expert pilots will do anything to destroy their enemies, no matter how silly.

FUN FACT
The handy Pig Empire symbol on the helmet reminds the pilots which side they are on—they keep forgetting!

Breather tubes are connected to a life-support pack.

Piggy ears are primed for any approaching X-wing Birdfighters.

Be alert
Only the most dedicated pigs become elite TIE fighter pilots. They are always on standby, ready to go into battle at any moment!

GREEDORK

Greedork is a vicious bounty hunter. The creepy criminal is sent all over the galaxy by Jabba the Hog on dastardly missions. Ruthless Greedork always brings home the bacon!

Good hearing helps out with bird hunting.

Sheer greed

Greedork enjoys his job, especially when he gets paid in junk food. The greedy bounty hunter always demands an enormous bag of tasty treats, which are usually eaten very quickly!

Snout sniffs out both bird targets and junk food.

EVER-HUNGRY BOUNTY HUNTER

DATA FILE

▷ **Home planet:**
Rodia

▷ **Special power:**
Finding his targets

▷ **Pig pal:**
Jabba the Hog

Hunting Ham

Greedork is usually sent to find rogues who have not kept their promises to Jabba the Hog. On one such mission Greedork's number one target is Ham Solo!

FUN FACT

Greedork grew up on Tatooine—his dad, from their home planet Rodia, was also a bounty hunter called Greedork the Elder!

Fast blast

In a beak-to-snout face-off, Ham's rapid reactions save the day. Ham blasts the unlucky hunter before he gets blasted himself, escaping from Greedork's grip!

WHAT DOES IT TAKE TO BE
A BOUNTY HUNTER?

Wear a tough helmet. You will need it if you crash into things as often as Boba does.

A jetpack is essential for bounty hunters. It gives you a lift if battle is wearing you down.

Be greedy! If you know you are being paid in junk food, you'll achieve anything to get it.

Show no mercy! Always take the biggest slice of the pizza when sharing.

It is easy to sniff out Ham Solo with this snout- and you can smell his pal Terebacca a mile away!

Unlikely as it may seem, Jawa Birds have some of the best business brains in the galaxy! These short but sharp Tatooine traders sell scrap and electronic goods. They have an eye for a bargain!

Jawa Birds never remove their hand-woven robes.

Under the hood

While everybody can see their bright yellow eyes and beaks, nobody outside their flock has ever seen what's hidden underneath a Jawa Bird's hood. And to be honest, no-one wants to!

Belt to carry tools and any scraps found while out scavenging.

Fun Fact

Jawa Birds are famous for smelling awful! Best hold your beak if you buy something from them!

Droid deal

To the Jawa Birds C-3PYOLK and R2-EGG2 are just a pair of rickety robots. So they are very pleased when they are able to sell the damaged droids to Red for a good price.

Data File

▶ **Home planet:**
Tatooine

▶ **Special skill:**
Business deals

▶ **Bird buddies:**
Other Jawa Birds

Jawa Birds travel slowly through the deserts of Tatooine on an enormous sand-crawler that they store all their junk in!

NABOO

Beautiful Naboo is a small planet with breathtaking scenery, fine cities, and peaceful villages. It is home to important figures such as Peckmé Amidala and Darth Swindle. The pigs would just love to get their hooves on this planet!

Check the weather forecast —it can rain on Naboo.

POTENTIAL PIG HIDING-PLACE AT FIVE O'CLOCK BEHIND STATUE. CHECK!

GUNGANS DON'T LIKE OUTSIDERS, SO DON'T EXPECT A WARM WELCOME!

Otah Gunga

Deep beneath a lake on Naboo is the secret city of Otah Gunga. Gungan birds, such as Jar Jar Wings, live here in huge bubbles that keep out the water.

Naboo has many kilometers of pretty, grassy plains with the odd ancient statue of great birds from the planet's past.

It took many birds to carve this magnificent statue.

The planet has several famous mountain ranges.

DARTH MOAR

This evil Sith Pig is totally crazy and scary at all times. Even his evil boss, Count Dodo, thinks he has anger issues. He exists only to fight Jedi Birds and spends all day practicing to be a mean machine.

Male Dathomir boars grow pointy horns.

Sith Pig

Count Dodo chose Darth Moar to be his apprentice because Moar was so mad, he would carry out the crazy missions even Dodo would not do! One day, Moar hopes to be a Sith Lard himself.

Moar's tattoos show he comes from the fierce Nightboar tribe.

EVIL LORD OF THE PORK

Super saber
Having a double blade means Moar can fight two Jedi at once, which is his idea of a nice, quiet afternoon.

DATA FILE
▶ **Home planet:**
Dathomir

▶ **Special skill:**
Lightsaber dueling

▶ **Awful ally:**
Count Dodo

A match for a master Jedi
Moar has trained his whole life to duel with Jedi Birds and he can even match highly skilled Quail-Gon. In fact, faced with Moar, Gon might soon be a goner!

FUN FACT
Moar was once cut in half by Obi-Wan Kaboomi, but was so angry about it, his rage kept him alive!

EVIL PIG ALLIANCES

Although you can never really trust anybody from the Pork Side, some of these baddies are actually good buddies! The pigs have paired up to form foul friendships, helping each other to achieve their evil ends!

Jabba and Boba Fatt

Boba is the top bounty hunter, Jabba is a gruesome crime lord. These vile villains really respect each other!

Zam Weasel and Jango Fatt

Zam and Jango are piggy partners-in-crime. The pair works well together on their wicked assassin missions!

Redkin and Darth Swindle

When Redkin is Swindle's apprentice, the Pig Lord is kept busy teaching him the ways of the Pork Side!

Of course, the best evil ally of all is Lard Vader. If you gain his respect, like Boba Fatt did, you will be one powerful porker (and you can pig out at his banquets)!

ZAM WEASEL
SLY SHAPE CHANGER

Sneaky Zam is the ultimate master of disguise: She is a shape-shifter who can change her looks to fool her enemies. Let's face it, anyone would want to change their appearance if they looked like Zam!

Zam uses headphones to listen to bad pop music.

Mission mix-up
Despite her cool powers, Zam's missions don't always go to plan, like when Jango Fatt hired her to zap Peckmé Amidala. When she failed, Jango zapped Zam instead!

All Zam's gear can stretch to fit her changes of form.

COUNT DODO
SINISTER SITH

Posh pig Count Dodo is one snooty swine! This proud porker was once a gentle Jedi until his love of serious snacking lured him to the Pork Side. Dodo's menacing mustache alone is enough to terrify most of his foes.

FUN FACT
Dodo secretly dreams of being the big cheese one day and becoming Emperor.

Powerful piggy

Lurking beneath that beardy old face is more Force power than most Jedi Birds can handle. Cunning Count Dodo is almost unbeatable in a duel!

DATA FILE

▶ **Homeworld:**
Serenno

▶ **Special skill:**
Force lightning

▶ **Pig pal:**
General Grunter

Dodo loves to polish his silver cloak clasp until it shines.

COPYPIGS
CLONED PIG SOLDIERS

Once you've seen one Copypig, you've seen them all! These identical Pigtroopers were created by the Pork Side to build up a big army for invading planets and fighting wars.

Not clever clones

Copypigs have brawn rather than brains— they are trained to do nothing but fight. They grow up to be fearless and keen to serve the Pork Side!

Wide viewer gives pigs clearer sight.

All armor is identical— Copypigs hate to stand out from the crowd.

FUN FACT

Copypigs are all cloned and created on the planet of Kamino. They are clones of Jango Fatt!

MYNHOGS
ENERGY-ZAPPING PARASITE PIGS

Pesky Mynhogs are a cross between pigs and bats. These exceptionally annoying animals fly through space and attach themselves to spaceships, then start to suck out the power. Mynhogs just love eating energy!

King Mynhog

The Mynhogs all follow their monarch, King Mynhog. His Royal Nuisance is always first in line for some juicy ship energy—that's why he's so fat!

Wings hook onto spaceships so the Mynhog can hang around!

Beady eyes try to spot electric cables to snack on.

DATA FILE

▷ **Home planet:**
Unknown

▷ **Special skill:**
Leaching energy

▷ **Pig pals:**
Nobody likes Mynhogs!

PIG STAR

It's easily the most evil piggy plot yet! Loathsome Darth Swindle has made a vast vessel—the Pig Star—which can zap an entire planet! The Bird Rebels must destroy this moon-sized space station at all costs...

Red alert! Red Skywalker is all set to pilot his X-wing Birdfighter on a mission to destroy the Pig Star.

On this mission, Red is helped by his brave co-pilot R2-EGG2.

Destruction!

A laser blast from the *Mighty Falcon* distracts Lard Vader. This enables Red to shoot a torpedo into the heart of the Pig Star and make it explode. Red uses the power of the Force to hit his target.

LET'S GO THE WHOLE HOG AND DESTROY THAT THING!

Pigtroopers control the gun turrets to shoot down birds.

USE THE FORCE, RED, USE THE FORCE!

The trench floor has many different obstacles.

What does it take to be The Leader of the Pig Empire?

> Don't be an angry Jedi Bird- Come over to the Pork Side! Hot dog, anyone?

Make sure you have hundreds of Pigtroopers. They must be stupid and do anything you tell them.

Height can be intimidating. If you are not tall enough to tower over the birds, stand on a few Pigtroopers.

Have a big appetite. The more junk food you can pig out on, the more you belong to the Pork Side!

Practice heavy breathing. It makes you sound creepy and frightens your feathered Jedi foes!

GENERAL GRUNTER
CYBORG WARRIOR

This cyborg works for the pigs, but is actually a reptile underneath the mask. Grunter was blown to pieces in a spaceship years ago and rebuilt by Count Dodo. It was dastardly Dodo who blew him up in the first place!

DATA FILE

▷ **Homeworld:**
Kalee

▷ **Special skill:**
Cyborg power

▷ **Pig pal:**
Count Dodo

General Destruction

Ghastly Grunter is the most feared general of the Pork Side. He is famous for his nasty cough, which makes it impossible for him to creep up on anyone!

Lightsaber blades can be whirled to strike 20 times a second.

Reptile eyes do not miss a trick and can spot a Jedi Bird from miles away.

BATTLE PIGS
DROID DIMWITS

Designed to have all the best qualities of a real pig, these robot-swine somehow ended up with the worst! They are all connected and can act with one mind—unfortunately for them, it is a very stupid one!

FUN FACT
Not only do these droids get bashed up by the birds, but General Grunter also whacks them when they fail a mission!

Vocoder voice box enables them to moan constantly.

Computerized minds are linked to the main computer.

Terrible tactics
These dumb droids will walk straight into enemy fire with no idea of taking cover. Even the Jedi Birds get bored of using them for target practice.

DARTH SWINDLE

FIGHTS FOR:
The Pork Side

STRENGTHS:
Swindle is a good match for Yoda Bird. He is very strong in the Force and can hurl objects across a room with a little concentration!

WEAKNESSES:
During any duel Swindle seems to spend half his time cackling loudly. Sometimes he even distracts himself from the job in hand!

YODA BIRD

FIGHTS FOR:
The Jedi Birds

STRENGTHS:
Yoda's light body means that he is ultra-quick with his lightsaber and can dodge anything Swindle throws at him.

WEAKNESSES:
This wise bird often has his mind on higher things, so sometimes forgets the basics—like where he left his lightsaber!

WARHOGS
SHAPE-SHIFTING BATTLE DROIDS

The last thing a Bird Rebel wants is a Warhog hogging the limelight in battle. These deadly droids can change shape, and boast an awesome arsenal of weapons. Even Jedi Birds fear them!

FUN FACT
The Warhog can uncoil itself from the wheel position within seconds! Yikes!

The head area lowers to form part of the wheel.

Hog roll
One of the Warhog's sneakiest tricks is an ability to transform into a wheel-shape and then roll along at high speed. This is handy for making a fast getaway, or chasing down retreating birds.

These powerful missiles are deadly!

HOG GUARD
FEARED FIENDS WITH FORKS

The Hog Guard are Emperor Piglatine's personal protectors. They are tough and fiercely loyal to the Emperor—armed and ready to defend him with the prongs of their ultra-sharp forks!

Red heads

The Hog Guard are covered ear to hoof in bright red robes and helmets. Underneath their robes they have more body armor, which is, of course, red.

Crimson helmets are always polished and shiny.

FUN FACT

Piglatine selects only the most skillful and gifted pigs to be members of his Hog Guard.

Spiked forks can pierce almost anything!

WHAT DOES IT TAKE TO BE
A SITH APPRENTICE?

Act crazy. Some fierce red and black face tattoos will make you appear unstoppable.

Use a double-bladed lightsaber. The Jedi Birds use single blades—why fight fair?

Always obey your master. Especially if he is even scarier than you.

WHAT DO YOU WANT? MOAR! WHEN DO YOU WANT IT? NOW!

Follow the Pork Side.
Always pig out on junk food between meals!

GRAND MOFF TARKIN
PIG STAR COMMANDER

Pig Star top porker Grand Moff Tarkin has some grand ideas on how to build up the power of the Pig Empire. The cruel commander scares the birds senseless by threatening to blow up their planets!

FUN FACT
Grand Moff Tarkin has the biggest and bushiest mustache out of all the Pig Star crew!

Military boar
Old soldier Grand Moff is always alert—even his bristly eyebrows stand to attention. It was "the Moff" who planned the Pig Star and was in charge of building it!

Tarkin has won many medals, mostly awarded by himself!

TUSKEN RAIDERS
SINISTER DESERT SWINE

Tusken Raiders are dangerous desert-dwelling pigs who travel round the remotest areas of the planet Tatooine. They are well-known for creeping up on birds and suddenly attacking them!

Raid on Red

The creepy Tusken Raiders even try to ambush Red Skywalker. It's lucky that Obi-Wan Kaboomi is around to rescue him!

Lens protects sensitive eyes from the sand and attacks.

Sun block

Tusken Raiders are not the most stylishly dressed pigs! However, their heavy robes and bandages protect them from the harsh sun of the Tatooine desert.

Bandages stop delicate pig skin from turning into roast pork.

REDKIN SKYWALKER

LIKES:

Flying vehicles at great speed and preferably into unnecessary danger.

Doing the opposite of what Obi-Wan tells him. It's fun to drive your wise master nuts once in a while!

HATES:

Always having to use his powers to seek peace. Jedi are great fighters—why can't they just show those pigs who's the boss?

PEOPLE SAY I AM THE CHOSEN ONE—IT SOUNDS PRETTY COOL, WHATEVER IT MEANS!

RED SKYWALKER

LIKES:

Fighting the Pig Empire—it sure beats harvesting drips on the moisture farm on Tatooine.

Blowing up giant enemy space stations—bring them on!

HATES:

Chuck "Ham" Solo showing off all the time. He isn't even a Jedi!

Being left out of the action—going back to a quiet life on the Outer Rim is just not an option!

I WANT TO BE A JEDI, LEARN WISDOM, FIGHT EVIL, AND PLAY WITH COOL WEAPONS—JUST LIKE MY DAD!

131

QUIZ: WHICH JEDI BIRD ARE YOU?

START HERE

How often do you think about stuffing your face with junk food?

ALL DAY LONG

Forget being a Jedi, your destiny lies with the Pork Side!

NEVER

How long are you prepared to work towards being a Jedi Bird?

ER, YES ACTUALLY

Do you ever have evil thoughts of ruling the Universe?

NO, OF COURSE NOT!

YEARS AND YEARS

A FEW DAYS?

Do you enjoy sitting around thinking a lot, or going on dangerous missions against the Pork Side?

LIGHTSABER

Would you prefer to fight your enemy with a lightsaber or blow them up with a bomb?

You are an explosive Jedi Bird like Obi-Wan Kaboomi. You have got what it takes to be a great Jedi, but you do need to control those bombs!

BLOW IT UP!

You are a confused Jedi Bird like Redkin. If you cannot make up your mind, you are ripe to be recruited by the Pork Side!

You are an adventurous Jedi Bird like Quail-Gon. The more death-defying action the better, but take care!

You are a young enthusiastic Jedi Bird like Red. You are always raring to go, but just need to learn the patience of a Padawan.

EXTREME DANGER!

THAT'S A SILLY QUESTION!

And just exactly *how* dangerous do you like your missions?

NO! BRING ON THE ACTION!

You are a serious Jedi Bird like Moa Windu. You are very well respected amongst the other Jedi Birds, but you could smile a bit more!

SIT AND THINK

You are a wise Jedi Bird like Yoda. You can master the Force with the power of your mind, but nobody understands what you are saying!

Boba Fatt

Ruthless bounty hunter Boba is specially trained to hunt birds by zooming around with his jetpack to track them down. Unfortunately, braking is not his strong point, which can result in a sore snout!

Helmet conceals computer with mission data.

Daddy's boy

Boba is a perfect clone of his father, Jango. As well as sharing his love for candy, Boba has also inherited Jango's awesome spaceship and his terrifying arsenal of way-out weapons.

Boba hides his face behind a helmet so he never has to wash it.

BIRDY HUNTER

Piggy payback

Brooding Boba is determined to seek revenge for his father's defeat at the hands of the Jedi Birds. This pig means business!

DATA FILE

▶ **Homeworld:**
Kamino

▶ **Special skill:**
Hunting and capturing

▶ **Pig pals:**
Jabba, Jango

So long, Solo

Boba's greatest achievement was his capture of Chuck "Ham" Solo, who was then frozen like a cheap dinner. But Chuck got away in the end!

PORK FEDERATION SHIP

The Pork Federation's most important vessels should be used for peaceful means only, but the Federation is secretly in league with the pigs. The ship is used for dastardly means—blocking off Naboo from the rest of the galaxy!

I AM GOING TO BLAST THIS SHIP TO PIECES! WOO HOO!

I AM NOT SURE I TRUST THESE PORK FEDERATION GUYS, OBI-WAN...

Piggy plot

Obi-Wan and Quail-Gon visit the Pork Federation ship to try and sort things out, not knowing that the pigs plot to destroy them! The plucky birds make a daring escape.

The Pork Federation is blocking the planet Naboo, so that nobody can visit or leave. These curly tailed creeps must be stopped!

Beautiful Naboo has been invaded!

Giant pig snout design

Entrance to the docking bay

AT-AT
HUGE BATTLE WALKER

The AT-AT Walker is one of most versatile vehicles in the Pork Federation. These huge machines lumber across all types of land, shooting enemies from their powerful laser cannons!

FUN FACT

Did you know that AT-AT stands for All Terrain Armored Transport?

The laser cannon can do some serious damage!

Piggy pilot

Each walker is driven by a porker. The specially picked Pigtrooper pilots have a rigorous training program. It's an honor to be chosen—driving an AT-AT Walker is where it's at!

AT-ST
TWO-LEGGED SCOUT WALKER

The two-legged AT-ST vehicle is ideal for pigs trying to snout out their enemies! Like the larger AT-ATs, the AT-ST can be maneuvered over most terrains, but at a faster marching pace.

The AT-ST can be a bumpy ride —hold on tight!

FUN FACT
You guessed it! AT-ST stands for All Terrain Scout Transport!

The blaster bolts can blast a hole in almost anything!

Walk the pork
It takes special skills to pilot an AT-ST. You need great control to balance the vehicle, and good reactions so you can hide. You also need a good aim to shoot out lethal blaster bolts!

QUIZ: WHICH PATH WILL YOU TAKE?

Will you be joining the birds or does your destiny lie with the Pork Side? Find out by testing your knowledge. Which of the following statements about the birds and the Pork Side are true or false? Get a point for each right answer. Whichever side you know more about shows your true path. **Good luck!**

THE BIRDS

TRUE OR FALSE?

1 Jar Jar Wings uses his tongue as a weapon against the pigs.

TRUE OR FALSE?

2 Yoda Bird was Obi-Wan Kaboomi's teacher when he was training to become a Jedi.

TRUE OR FALSE?

3 Yoda Bird spent many years on the planet Naboo hiding from the Pork Side.

TRUE OR FALSE?

4 Princess Stella has a special weapon that can disrupt fields of gravity.

TRUE OR FALSE?

5 Moa Windu holds the record for being the fastest flying bird in the galaxy.

TRUE OR FALSE?

6 The Blue Squadron pilot birds always fly in groups.

TRUE OR FALSE?

7 Terebacca is the singer in a rock band that regularly tours on Tatooine.

THE PORK SIDE

TRUE OR FALSE?

1 Darth Swindle can use the Force to send out lightning from his trotters!

TRUE OR FALSE?

2 Count Dodo helps to persuade Redkin to go over to the Pork Side.

TRUE OR FALSE?

3 Darth Moar has a special double-bladed lightsaber to fight with.

TRUE OR FALSE?

4 Lard Vader and his piggy forces invaded the icy wastelands of Cloud City.

TRUE OR FALSE?

5 The Pig Star can destroy another star with its laser weapon.

TRUE OR FALSE?

6 General Grunter is in charge of all the Battle Pigs.

TRUE OR FALSE?

7 Lard Vader has launched his own range of exclusive beauty and haircare products.

The Pork Side. 1. *TRUE!* **2.** *FALSE! Darth Swindle lured Redkin to the Pork Side.* **3.** *TRUE!* **4.** *FALSE! Lard Vader invaded Hoth.* **5.** *FALSE! The Pig Star destroy planets, not stars.* **6.** *TRUE!* **7.** *FALSE! Vader is not interested in beauty products!*

The Birds. 1. *TRUE!* **2.** *FALSE! Quail-Gon was Obi's teacher.* **3.** *FALSE! Yoda lived on Dagobah.* **4.** *TRUE!* **5.** *FALSE! Moa Windu cannot fly.* **6.** *TRUE!* **7.** *FALSE! Terebacco really cannot sing!*

141

INDEX

HEY, TERRY! WHEN DID YOU LAST HAVE A BIRDBATH? YOU COULD SCARE OFF THE PIGS WITH THAT SMELL!

AWAARWWWGGGG!
WAARGH!
AWAARWWWGGGG!

LONDON, NEW YORK, MUNICH,
MELBOURNE, and DELHI

DK LONDON
Senior Editor Sadie Smith
Editors Ruth Amos, Emma Grange,
Kathryn Hill, Julia March
Senior Designers Lisa Robb, Lynne Moulding
Designers Nick Avery, Richard Horsford, Toby Truphet
Pre-Production Producer Marc Staples
Senior Producer Danielle Smith
Managing Editor Laura Gilbert
Design Manager Maxine Pedliham
Art Director Ron Stobbart
Publishing Manager Julie Ferris
Publishing Director Simon Beecroft

This paperback edition published in the United States in 2014

First published in the United States in 2014 by DK Publishing,
345 Hudson Street, New York, New York 10014

002–196559–Feb/14

Page design copyright © 2014 Dorling Kindersley Limited
A Penguin Random House Company

DK books are available at special discounts when purchased in bulk for sales promotions,
premiums, fund-raising, or educational use. For details, contact: DK Publishing Special Markets,
345 Hudson Street, New York, New York 10014
SpecialSales@dk.com

A CIP catalog record for this book is available
from the Library of Congress

ISBN: 978-1-4654-2167-8

Color reproduction by Altaimage, UK
Printed and bound in China by South China Printing Company (LTD)

DK would like to thank Nita Ukkonen at Rovio, Jonathan Rinzler at Lucasfilm, Hilary Bird
for the index, Sam Bartlett for design assistance, and Laura Nickoll for proofreading.

Discover more at
www.dk.com

**NOW YOU HAVE THE
LOWDOWN ON THOSE
DASTARDLY PIGS AND VERY
ANGRY BIRDS!**